POPS!

Read more by Balaji Venkataramanan

Flat-track Bullies

Read more for middle-grade readers from Duckbill

Karma Fights a Monster by Evan Purcell
Karma Meets a Zombie by Evan Purcell
Ninja Nani and the Bumbling Burglars by Lavanya Karthik
Ninja Nani and the Zapped Zombie Kids by Lavanya Karthik
Ninja Nani and the Mad Mummy Mix-up by Lavanya Karthik
Against All Odds by Ramendra Kumar
The Case of the Candy Bandit by Archit Taneja
The Case of the Careless Aliens by Archit Taneja
Oops the Mighty Gurgle by RamG Vallath
The Deadly Royal Recipe by Ranjit Lal
Vanamala and the Cephalopod by Shalini Srinivasan
Neha and the Nose by Ruchika Chanana
Ravana Refuses to Die by Rustom Dadachanji
Simply Nanju by Zainab Sulaiman
Hot Chocolate is Thicker than Blood by Rupa Gulab
The Sherlock Holmes Connection by Martin Widmark, Anushka Ravishankar, Katarina Genar and Bikram Ghosh
Tiger Boy by Mitali Perkins
The Hill School Girls: Alone by A. Coven
The Hill School Girls: Secrets by A. Coven
The Hill School Girls: Strangers by A. Coven
The Hill School Girls: Trouble by A. Coven
The Piano: Story of a Friendship by Nandita Basu

POPS!

BALAJI VENKATARAMANAN

duckbill

An imprint of Penguin Random House

DUCKBILL BOOKS

USA | Canada | UK | Ireland | Australia
New Zealand | India | South Africa | China | Singapore

Duckbill Books is part of the Penguin Random House group of companies whose addresses can be found at global.penguinrandomhouse.com

Published by Penguin Random House India Pvt. Ltd
4th Floor, Capital Tower 1, MG Road,
Gurugram 122 002, Haryana, India

Penguin Random House India

First published by Duckbill Books 2019

This edition published in Duckbill Books by Penguin Random House India 2020

10 9 8 7 6 5 4 3 2

ISBN 9789387103146

Typeset by PrePSol Enterprises Pvt. Ltd.
Printed at Manipal Technologies Limited, India

www.penguin.co.in

MIX
Paper | Supporting responsible forestry
FSC® C043100

This is a legitimate digitally printed version of the book and therefore might not have certain extra finishing on the cover.

My name is V. Arun. I am seven years old.

My father's name is Venkatesh. He is very good. He never gets mad at me. He takes me to malls, where we play a lot of games. He buys me a lot of toys and chocolates. He got me this nice toy for my birthday. We watch movies and sports together. He teaches me cricket and car racing.

I love my father.

Me

That's the most I have bluffed in a day.

The thing is, I have never met my dad. I have never seen him except in the wedding album that Mom had shown me. He left us as soon as I was born.

It's like that story Paati told me the other day of how man started facing a lot of problems after he betrayed god in that garden. Maybe Mom or I bit a forbidden fruit or something, so Saturn or god decided to teach us a lesson, and we ended up this way.

Whenever my teacher or someone asks me, 'What does your father do?', I bluff and say that my father is in the US, working as an engineer.

I hate that question or any questions about him.

The moment I came home I tore the paper to bits. I hate the moral science period. I hate my dad. I hate him!

My Father

When I was much smaller, I believed Mom when she told me that my dad was away on work and that he would be back with loads and loads of chocolates and toys.

Every night at bedtime, I used to ask Mom to tell me stories about Dad working really hard in a faraway land and making lots of money and buying me lots and lots of stuff.

'Will he buy me a toy scooter?'

'Yes.'

'Will he buy me a mini car? '

'Yes.'

'Will he buy me Nike shoes? '

'Yes.'

I would keep on and on asking, and the next thing I knew, it would be morning, because both of us had fallen asleep.

I used to dream of Dad visiting me with all the goodies.

I kept asking Mom, 'When will he come back?'

'During your summer vacation.'

And during the vacation—'Oh, your father is busy. He will come next year ...'

LKG, UKG, first grade, second grade, Dad didn't turn up.

For Christmas and Diwali, Mom gave me gifts and said that Dad had given them through Santa.

'My dad, he's the busiest man in the world,' I thought.

And then Mama was crying one day. She told me, 'Dad won't come back to us. He is gone, forever!'

I didn't understand what it meant and kept asking questions.

'Why, is he angry with us?'

'Yeah.'

'Why?'

'Because he doesn't like us.'

'Why?'

'Because he wants to live away from us.'

'Why?'

I kept asking why, again and again, but I didn't even listen to Mom's answers.

All I had in my mind was 'Why, why, why?'

The toy cars and chocolates were melting away like ice cream.

At first, I thought Mom was playing some kind of April-fool joke, but she cried a lot and I sort of understood it was for real.

Mom told me not to talk about it at school, and to tell my friends that my dad's working in America as a computer engineer. And to this day, that's what I tell my friends and teachers.

'Is lying not wrong, Ma? Won't god punish me?'

'Yes, it's wrong, Arun. But I think god will understand.'

Mom

God may have given me a monster dad. But then, I have the sweetest mom in the world.

If I have to write about my mom, I can go on for pages and pages.

She works in this big computer company, and she earns a lot of money. We even have a car. Yeah, I even went to Singapore with Mom and my grandparents, last summer vacation.

That was the first time I had ever been on a plane. Boy, how I loved it! Of course I took the window seat. I thought there would be a lot of noise inside the plane, like the noise we hear when the plane flies right above us, but actually, there was very little noise.

Mom and I kept smiling at each other as the plane took off and the lights got dimmed, and Mom held my hand hard. I guess she's scared of planes. Mom had told me that my ears would start paining when the plane took off. But I didn't feel any pain. She held her ears and smiled at me. It was really nice.

We glanced over at Paati and she was praying as the plane took off. Very funny!

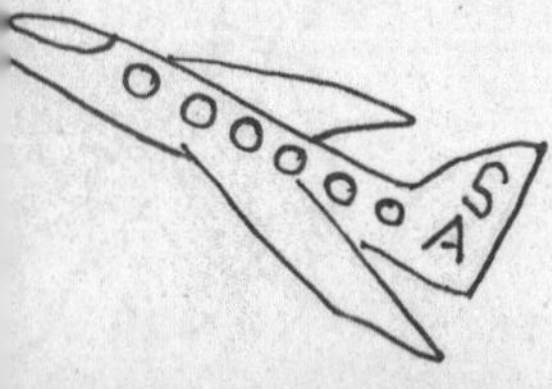

They started serving dinner immediately after the plane stopped wobbling after the takeoff. I guess if you buy an air ticket, they give free food. They served upma and surprisingly, it tasted yummy.

'Arun, you don't even touch upma when we have it at home,' Mom remarked.

'But then, yours is not as tasty as this.'

I opened the book they keep behind every seat. I found burgers and cola and lots of stuff that was for sale ...

'Ma, I am still feeling hungry, can we buy a burger and cola? Let's share it. Fifty-fifty.'

Mom took the book and put it back in the pouch.

'Just close your eyes and go to sleep. By the time you wake up, we will be in Singapore.'

'Singapore is foreign, right?' I checked with Mom again

'Yeah, it's a foreign country.'

'Then I can go tell my friends at school that I went to a foreign country for summer holidays.'

'You certainly can.'

We stayed in Shanthi Aunty's house with this huge window, on the twenty-seventh floor or something. I spent a lot of time looking at the huge buildings,

wondering at how small the kids playing on the ground appeared. Surely, if Spiderman was around in Singapore, he would love to glide from one building to the other. I tried shooting imaginary webs towards distant buildings just the way Spiderman does.

My aunt and uncle kept laughing at me, but I didn't care.

'Ma, I think we can even do bungee jumping from this height.'

'You'd better move away from the window before you start getting crazier ideas,' Taatha remarked, and everyone went ha-ha-ha.

We went to the Sentosa Island where we rode in the rope car and to the Bird Park and the Night Safari at the zoo. It was super fun.

They take you around the zoo in this open top van through the lions' area, elephants' place, tigers' den and leopards' lair. The lions roared hungrily, while a herd of elephants were having some meeting or something in the centre of the ground. An elephant with huge tusks was chained to a massive tree. Its tusks shone in the moonlight.

'Why is only that elephant chained, Ma?'

'Ask that guide?' Mom laughed.

I was kinda scared.

'I think that elephant has done something bad. He has been given some punishment.'

As we reached the leopards' lair, the guide announced that there was a gift for the person who spotted the leopard first. Immediately, everyone looked into the enclosure to see where it was hiding. There were bushes all around and a small pond and a deep pit running right around the fence to prevent the leopard from jumping over.

'It is there, Ma. On top of that tree, on that branch. Look! Look there! See its tail's hanging down!' I shouted. Yeah, I have seen on Discovery Channel. The leopards generally sleep on top of the trees.

'Excellent, son! You are a very smart guy,' said the guide, and all the people around clapped.

Ma beamed with pride.

'When will I get the gift, Ma?' I asked Mom, and the person next to me laughed and repeated my question to the guide.

'Oh, you can collect it at the information centre right after the safari,' he announced.

Mom kissed me as soon as everyone turned away.

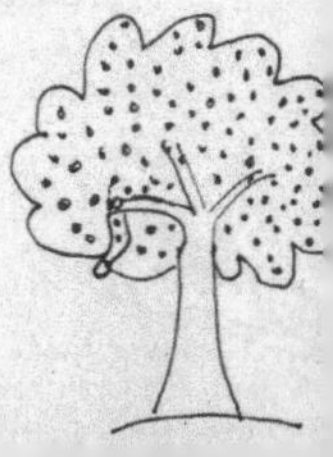

Mom is strict and all with my studies. The first thing she asks Paati and Pa after reaching home is if I have completed my homework.

Yeah, mostly its Paati and Pa who help me out with my homework; Mom's busy, you know. But then she gets me ice cream (she likes ice cream, too), and lots of toys. I even got a pair of Nike shoes two weeks back, the ones with orange laces.

Though she yells a lot at me, she doesn't spank me and all, even if I am up to some mischief—like if I come up with a lame excuse to skip school or if I don't finish my lunch or something like that.

She cries a lot some days. I really feel sorry for her and mad at my dad.

At night, she tells me everything that has happened at her office and I tell her about my day at school.

She's very nice. I can't understand why my dad didn't like her.

I have asked her a thousand times about it.

But she just says, 'I don't know.'

'Arun, no more of that discussion here; your father is not a good man,' Taatha cut me off one day and Mom too was silent.

So, I guess that's the truth.

Once I grow big, I am going to make Mom proud by becoming a successful astronaut or something.

In the past couple of months, she seems happier, after she met this friend at work.

I am very happy for her.

Know what, Mom is a very good dancer. During the weekends, if Mom's in a good mood, we just switch on the TV and dance to the movie songs. Yeah, Mom and I.

We watch the dance moves of the stars on the TV and follow the steps. Sometimes Mom teaches me the steps and sometimes I teach her.

We just keep going on and on. It makes both of us happy.

Paati and Pa laugh their hearts out seeing us dance.

I sometimes make Paati or Pa dance along with us. It is all very funny, you know.

'I think we need to do it every day, that way I'll get to exercise regularly,' Mom says.

'Yeah, let's do it every day, Ma.'

But then, on weekdays, she comes home quite late and is very tired.

Yeah, we have some really happy weekends. And then, one weekend, we went to the Family Court.

The Court

I knew that it would not be a good day the moment I saw a single black crow on the electric post opposite the bedroom window.

Yeah, two for joy! One for sorrow! I quickly crossed my eyes and looked at the crow so that it would look like there were two there. Two for joy, I tried telling myself. But then, you know.

It turned out to be a really weird day.

I met my father for the first time in my life, at the court.

Mom asked me to dress up, in the morning.

'But it's Saturday, Ma, I want to sleep for some more time.'

On weekdays, you know, I wake up at 6.30 am. Most times before Mom does. Taatha wakes me up after he has had his morning coffee.

'Pa, I will get up after Ma,' I tell him.

'No Arun, your van will come in half an hour.'

Why can't the schools start late, like Mom's office?

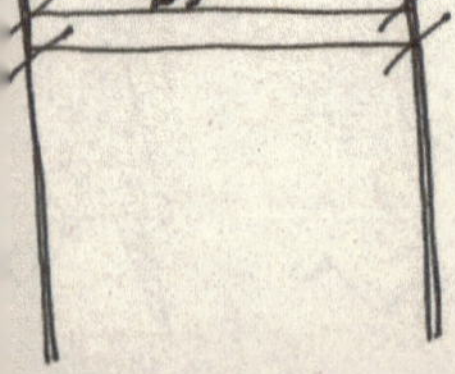

'Arun, we need to start early. Get up now.' Ma disturbed my sleep again.

'Where are we going, Ma?'

'To the court.'

That's the first time I heard Mom say the word 'court'. I got up immediately.

'Why?'

'We are going to meet your dad.'

My whole body started shivering and it felt like I was getting a fever or something.

'I-I-I don't want to meet him.'

Before we left, Paati and Pa told me a million times, 'Don't call him Appa. Never tell him anything happening back at home if he asks something about your mother. Never accept any eatables from him. Never bring anything given by him into this house. If he asks anything about Ma, say, I don't know. Cry, shout "Police! Police!" if he tries taking you away with him.'

I didn't know why they were saying all this to me.

'Don't worry, Arun. You will be fine. I will be there with you,' Mom comforted me, when I started crying.

She too wiped tears from her eyes.

'Ma, didn't you tell me the other day that you would enrol me in karate classes?' I started crying again.

'What to do, sweetie? I'll enrol you for the Sunday batch.'

'But there is no Sunday batch!'

'No, there is one, Arun.'

'No! I want to get a black belt soon!'

'You already have a black belt,' Mom tried to joke even though her face was sad.

When I was in the first standard, I had seen this video of a kid breaking bricks with bare hands, and I tried doing the same on the dining table at home. The next thing I knew, my hand had swollen up and I had to wear a bandage for a month.

Yeah, I told myself that day, I would take revenge on the table by smashing it to pieces after learning karate. You wicked dining table!

And now I can't go to karate class.

At the Family Court, the judge, a lady in black clothes, asked Mom to take me to some room. I thought it would be like a classroom or hospital ward or something. I said that I didn't want to go there. But then Mom said that we didn't have a choice.

What to do?

We walked into a big hall. It was like a playroom with a lot of animals painted on the walls. There was this tree with a monkey hanging upside down and a cobra sunbathing in one of the branches. There was a giraffe, an elephant grazing and a tiger drinking water from the river. There was even this leopard lazing on top of a branch, just like the one I had seen in the Singapore zoo. There were a lot of stuffed toys—a lion, a turtle and Winnie the Pooh—and there was even a slide and a small swing. I liked the slide the most.

The room was actually okay. But then, the people there were not. Some looked very happy while some looked very sad.

There was this kid who kept looking at me from the moment I walked in, and another who was busy playing with a helicopter. There was this small girl and her mom, each with a book in hand, busy reading. Then there was this guy with a running nose who had come with his grandmom. He was lying on the sofa with his legs on his granny's lap. There was this lady busy with her laptop and her son equally busy with a pack of chips.

There was a policewoman keeping a watch on everyone. I wondered why.

I hated the place the moment I walked in, though it had a lot of toys and all.

'That's your father.' Mom pointed to a man standing in the corner. He started coming towards us even before she could finish the sentence.

I was mighty scared as the man walked towards me.

Mom had shown me their wedding photo, but he looked different in that. This guy had a beard. I am generally scared of men with beards. To make it scarier, the man's thick moustache was twirled at the ends. Yeah, menacing!

He had a backpack that he dropped on the floor, as soon as he saw me. He had longer hair than in that photo and his eyes were brown, unlike Mom's, which are jet black.

I hesitated to go near him.

Mom said, 'I will wait here, go meet him.'

I told her, 'Don't go anywhere, I am scared, Ma, I am scared, Ma.' I tried pulling her hand.

But she had already moved a couple of steps back.

And there he was. The Man. Standing right above me.

I stood like this deer in front of a tiger in that Discovery Channel video.

Mom's right, the Man's stupid. He's kind of weird. He ran his hand over my head and then started smelling my hair. Sniff-sniff-sniff!

He kept his palm on mine.

'You have big fingers.'

That's the first thing he ever said to me.

'You will be able to bowl fast like Shoaib Akhtar.'

That's the second thing he said to me, though I didn't know who Shoaib Akhtar was.

'No, your fingers are stubby. You will be able to bowl like Shane Warne,' he continued. He looked me up and down. 'You are up to my waist. I think you will grow taller than me.'

He wasn't very tall, but when he held my fingers his hands seemed very firm, like a clamp or something. He felt my cheek where there was a rash. He asked if Mom had taken me to the doctor to have it examined. He then touched my ears; 'Just like mine,' he muttered and pulled them playfully. I didn't like it at all.

He then went to everyone in the room taking me along with him. 'My son! My son!' he kept saying. As if I was a trophy or something. Stupid man!

I didn't want to go with him, but he looked menacing; what if he slapped me or something?

He tried lifting me with one hand but he couldn't.

'You probably weigh more than 25 kgs I guess, you fat little boy,' he laughed at me. He then tried lifting me with both hands and grunted loudly with the effort. 'Umm!'

I hated him like hell. I hate it when someone calls me fat.

The Man offered me chocolates, which I didn't accept. I looked at Mom, who was standing a little away, watching us.

Mom nodded at me to accept and I stretched out my hand.

'Which ones do you like? Dairy Milk or 5 Star?'

I didn't answer him. The fact is, I like all chocolates. It doesn't matter if it is a 5 Star or Dairy Milk.

The judge at the court has told Mom to bring me to the court, I mean, to this children's centre, once every month. So it's gonna be torture the first Saturday of every month.

He wasn't bad to me or anything. But I didn't like it.

I don't like meeting him.

Do I have a choice?

The Man

Know what, the Man showed up at the school gates today. As I got down from the van, he held out his hand. For a moment, it felt as if my heart would come out of my mouth.

Neither Ma nor Taatha nor Paati had prepared me for this.

I put my head down and ran into the school, though he kept calling out my name, 'Arun, Arun!'

I thought he would come running behind me, but then he stopped at the gates.

I couldn't concentrate in class.

I kept thinking, will he be standing outside when I walk back to the van? Will he kidnap me and take me to his house?

The moment I stepped out of the school gate, I dashed to the van. Once in, I looked around, but he wasn't there in the evening.

The moment I reached home, I told Mom and Taatha about it.

Mom, Paati and Pa asked me everything the Man had said to me.

Paati said, 'For your own good, don't pay attention to whatever that man says.'

'We should lodge a police complaint immediately. He can be charged with anything—kidnapping, stalking, scaring a kid, just anything,' Taatha said.

Mom wanted to wait and watch.

When I told them I hated meeting the Man, Paati asked Mom, 'Why should we put our child through all this stress of meeting that monster?'

Mom's friend comes home to pick Mom up every morning on his way to the office.

I think the Man doesn't have a job. Otherwise, who would hang around at the school gates, that too in the morning, right?

Nightmares

I have been getting nightmares ever since I met the Man.

This morning I woke up crying, 'Leave me, leave me. Don't take me away. I don't want to leave Ma!'

I had this bad dream of the Man taking me away, just like Ravana took away Sita. Though Mom laughed, Paati shouted that the Man was evil and must have cast some spell on me.

Mom said, 'Don't be stupid.'

Paati shouted at her. 'See, he is unable to sleep. I've been telling you right from the beginning that it is a bad idea to allow that man to establish contact with Arun.'

Even at school, I felt scared as hell today. The Man had come today as well. Standing in the same place as yesterday and calling out: 'Arun, Arun.'

Our class teacher Anita Ma'am had asked me why my dad didn't turn up for the PTA meetings. I told her that he was in the US.

But then Ma'am didn't leave it at that. She asked, 'Where in the US?'

Actually, I don't really know any place there, so I told her, 'In the biggest city of America.'

She asked, 'Is he in New York?' And I nodded my head.

Nonsense!

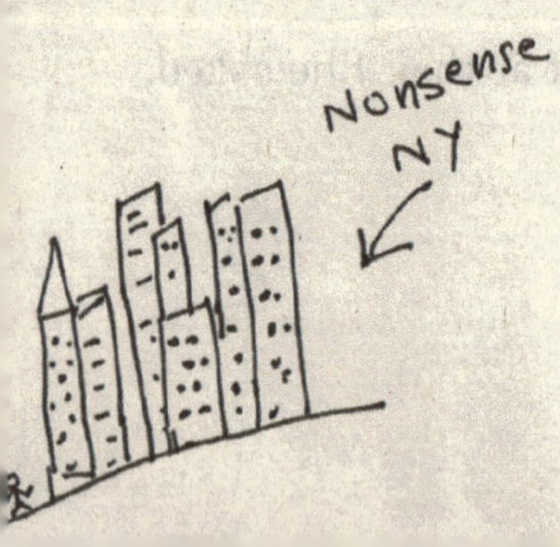

Pop

On my second visit to the court, the Man brought chocolates. Though I love chocolates more than anything else and would have cleaned up everything if given a chance, I said no.

'Fat little boy,' he called me.

'I don't like it when someone calls me fat,' I told him rudely.

Actually, Taatha had told me that I needn't be nice to him at all, and if I behaved rudely, he would stop coming to see me.

'Okay, okay, call me Dad. Can you call me Dad?' He mock-punched me.

I kept staring at the peacock on the wall and at the lady and the girl who were busy reading again. They simply keep reading and reading, like forever. I haven't seen the girl's father or even seen her talking to her mom.

'Or call me Pops,' he continued. 'Pop as in Poppins. Pop as in popcorn. Pop as in Popeye the Sailor. Do you know Popeye the Sailor?'

He brought me this bicycle.

In fact, I had been asking Mom to get me one. She had said, 'You do well in the half-yearly exams and I will get you one.'

It was red, my favourite colour. It had a bell on the left handle and even a small headlight. How did he bring it all the way to the court on his bike? Or did he ride it all the way? That's not possible, right?

I acted as if I was totally disinterested in the cycle. To be quite frank, I wanted to cycle around, but then, Mom was watching me closely.

The other kids approached the cycle. I hated it like hell. But, as they were hesitating, the Man just nodded to the kids to try it out.

A kid kept cycling around the room and I kept looking at the wall, though the Man was sitting right next to me on the sofa, trying to talk to me.

The Man kept annoying me. The moment I turned his way, he would go, 'Pop! Pop! Pop!'

He made a gun shape with his hand and put it to my head and said, 'Pop! Pop! Pop!'

Very annoying!

'Do you know to ride a cycle?'

I just kept looking away.

'Once you know how to ride, you can ride through your street. Vroom! Vroom!'

Just then, Running Nose tried riding the cycle without holding the handlebar and boom! He hit the wall smack and fell down. Both the Man and I ran towards the cycle. The headlight had been shattered. Oh, how much I loved that headlight!

But the Man, instead of checking the cycle, was busy checking the boy who was crying, holding his knee.

'Nothing, boss! Get up, sir! You rode like a champion. Now let's clap for our champion rider!' He turned towards the other kids. And everyone around clapped.

I don't think he is a champion rider or anything.

'Do you have a chocolate? You? You?' he checked with the kids around. They just shook their heads. But the boy wouldn't stop crying. He wailed, clutching his knee.

The Man blew a big bubble with the chewing gum in his mouth at Running Nose and handed a stick of gum to him. I mean, sugar-free chewing gum! SUGAR-FREE! Nobody gives kids sugar-free chewing gum, right? The packet clearly had the warning: 'Not recommended for children'. Mom had shown me the other day. And still this Man gave it to the kid. I completely agree with Taatha—he is a dummy head.

Mom always says that if you swallow chewing gum, it will get stuck to your heart and give you a heart attack. I never eat chewing gum.

But the kid was beaming now, chewing hard at the gum and know what? His mom too was laughing instead of getting mad at the Man who had given a sugar-free gum to her son.

There was a pair of twins with Bugs Bunny teeth there. One of them tried putting his hand into the Man's pocket to take out a chewing gum stick but the Man just shook his head vigorously at the kid.

'Please, please,' the Rabbit-tooth Twin pleaded.

'N-O,' the Man shook his head again.

He then blew a big bubble, looking at me.

'This is how you blow a bubble.' He rolled his tongue around the gum and then blew air.

The bubble burst and he went 'Pop! Pop! Pop!'

'Do you want to try?'

I didn't answer his question.

His friends (I mean the other guys there) came over and tried speaking to me. I didn't really care. I looked at Mom and she just nodded her head.

The Man told me he is going to join my school as a student. I ignored his boring talk again.

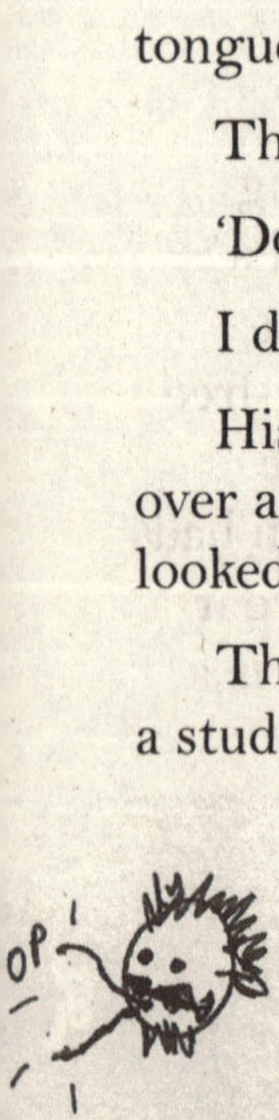

'Want to see a trick?' He snapped his fingers.

'Come on, stretch your hand and touch that wall. Now snap your fingers a couple of times and bingo! Your hand will become short. See, it won't reach the wall. Every single time. It's a challenge!' He snapped his fingers and stretched his hand out again and yeah, his hand did appear to get short.

He taught this trick to the other kids there, and soon the whole place was filled with the sound of snapping fingers.

The kids were showing off this trick to their mothers, who were smiling at them and then glancing at the Man.

'If you want it to get even shorter, snap your fingers thrice instead of twice and chant this mantra: Pops! Pops! Pops!' He laughed mischievously.

I simply ignored him and looked at Mom. She was expressionless.

Back home, Mom and Paati wanted to know everything the Man had said to me.

As usual, I told them everything.

'Did he ask about Mom?'

'No.'

'Did he ask about us?' asked Paati.

'No.'

'Did he ask you to go along with him?'

'No.'

'Ma, that Running Nose is going to have a heart attack today, isn't he?' I checked with Mom.

'I am not sure if that boy is going to have a heart attack, but one of us is surely going to get one if you and your mother keep going to that children's centre every month.' It was Paati, and we all laughed along.

After dinner, while brushing my teeth (yeah, I brush twice a day), I looked at the mirror and stretched my hand towards it and moved back till I was just touching it with my fingers.

I did a couple of quick snaps with my fingers and stretched my hand again.

Oh yeah, it didn't reach the mirror anymore. WOW!

Would my hand get even shorter, if I uttered the mantra 'Pops! Pops! Pops!', I wondered. But I couldn't see any difference.

The next morning, the whole class was snapping around. Even Rohit, who generally doesn't talk to me, was snapping his fingers.

Ramesh even showed the trick to our class teacher.

'Come on, show it again,' she asked him. Rohit did it again. 'Wow! Who taught you this?'

'Arun.'

'Who taught you this trick, Arun?' she asked me.

'Taatha,' I bluffed.

'Cool trick.'

'Ma'am, why does our hand get short after snapping our fingers?' Rani asked Ma'am.

Ma'am looked at me.

I shook my head.

'You should ask your Taatha about it,' she smiled.

Suddenly, I became cool. This is the first time this has happened to me in my class.

Should I tell Ma'am that the Man taught me this?

Obviously, I can't ask Mom or Taatha why my hand gets shorter when I snap my fingers.

Should I tell Ma'am to wait until next month, I mean the first Saturday, for the answer?

I'm sure the Man won't know the answer either.

Soon even Ma'am had joined everyone and was snapping her fingers.

I have been snapping my fingers all day. The only thing I am worried about now is, will my hand get shorter and shorter and end up being as short as a fairy's wing?

Does it also work with the legs? Let me try ...

Monkey Tricks

I think the Man is an auto-mechanic or something. He comes on a different bike every day to school. Yesterday, it was an ordinary bike. Today, it is a Bullet. I like the Bullet, especially the sound of it.

Dub-dub-dub-dub!

He just keeps smiling at me. Though I ignore him, he still smiles.

I sometimes think he keeps smiling like that even in his sleep.

I told Taatha that the Man has been standing outside the school gate every day and that he jumps when he sees me and that he does monkey tricks.

You know, Taatha doesn't laugh much. I guess he thinks smiling is bad for health or something. But then, hearing this, he laughed his pants off.

Reported

Mom and Taatha came to school today. They saw the Man standing in a corner.

I smiled a sly smile in his direction. He smiled brightly as usual. Since he is not smart, I guess he didn't realise that he was going to be reported today.

Mom complained and the watchman pushed the Man physically as he tried to come forward. Yeah, it was scary. It kinda felt bad; a big man being pushed by another.

'You do it one more time and I will flatten you. Who gave you the authority to push someone like that?' the Man warned the watchman, who immediately backed away.

I was happy that the Man shouted at the watchman; that watchman, he teases me and calls me 'Sumo' all the time.

A small crowd had gathered at the gate by now. My classmate Krishna's mom was also there and my vanmates as well.

Mom met the school principal, who called up the police.

A policeman came. He had a lengthy discussion with the Man. Then the Man had a heated discussion with the principal, to my surprise, in English.

He really speaks English very well actually, better than Mom or anybody that I know; even better than Mom's friend.

Taatha interrupted both of them repeatedly and the principal cut him off saying, 'We are discussing this, right? You can leave now.'

The policeman then took the Man aside and they both walked away together.

Is the policeman going to put the Man behind bars? Have I made a mistake?

No, I don't think he will be imprisoned, because I thought of the number eight and flipped open a page in my maths book—it was not eight. My friend taught me this game, and it always works.

Mom was really mad today as the Man had embarrassed her in public. She sat on the chair while Paati and Pa stood around her. Paati tried rubbing her hair.

'Why the hell should he create a scene at school? He doesn't want us to live in peace,' she cried.

Taatha wanted to file a case right away.

I felt bad for Mom, for all the troubles today. I felt bad because now my teachers, my friends and everyone else knows my story.

Nobody talked to me in class today.

'My father is in the US,' I used to say. I don't think I can say that anymore.

But I kinda felt bad for the Man as he has never really troubled me. He just does his thing and goes away.

I think the Man is not an auto-mechanic who works in some garage. I don't think a mechanic speaks English this well, right? The auto-mechanics near my house don't speak English at all.

Basketball

The Man has not been put in jail. He has somehow gained entry into the school. I think he did some magic and gained entry. Or, as Paati says, he probably cast a spell on the principal.

He was playing basketball with the PT Sir and a few other high-school boys this morning. I mean, really tall boys.

You know, our PT Sir never talks to boys who are not good at sports, except to shout at them or if their hair is too long or something. I don't know why he talked with the Man.

He threw the basketball to him.

Boy, the Man plays like an actual basketball player. He shoots accurately from almost the half-line. He really can play.

He winked at me as I went into the class.

The Maths Ma'am, who now knows that the Man is my dad, kept asking questions.

'Where does he work? Where does he live? Is he staying alone? He plays basketball very well. Why don't you bring your dad to the PTA meeting?'

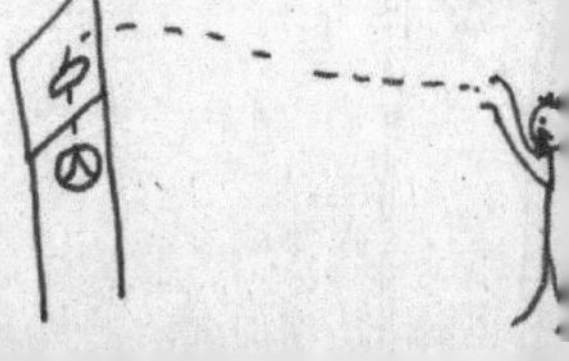

I heard her telling the ayah that I looked more like the Man and that he seemed a very nice guy.

'Is that your father?' my benchmate Ria asked me.

I kept looking at the blackboard.

After the first period, I peeped out, but then he wasn't there.

That evening, the watchman kept staring at me as I walked out of the gates.

Usually, every time I come out, he calls out 'Sumo!' But today, he just kept staring at me.

I could see fear in his eyes. Yes, FEAR!

Mom asked me what happened at school.

I said I had a headache and went to bed.

Clak! Clak!

I guess the man has very poor concentration.

Mom has filed a case that he has been following, threatening and scaring me.

Taatha told me to nod my head if the judge asked if I was feeling threatened.

And the court, it was nothing like the ones you see in the movies. It was this old building with this old hall where this judge in black robes sits on a podium and then everyone kinda stands around her.

One guy keeps calling out names and people move towards the podium and the men in black (I mean, the lawyers) keep addressing the judge as 'My lord, my lord.'

It's kinda hilarious, as if she is a god or something, right?

Everything is old about the place. Old tables, old clock, old papers, old lady judge and old men all around.

Okay, where was I? Yeah, the man has very poor concentration. I'm sure he must have been very bad at studies at school.

Unlike Mom, who was paying attention to the judge and to the clerk who was calling out the names, the Man just kept looking at me.

I turned in his direction and he winked at me. I immediately turned away.

When I stole a glance at him again, there he was, still looking at me. He winked again. He put his tongue against his cheek, as if his mouth was stuffed with this big toffee and kept signalling to me, asking if I wanted one.

I am not a little kid to be fooled by these tricks. Irritating!

The court hall is a boring room with no place to even sit. I asked for Mom's mobile but she wouldn't give it to me.

I glanced at him and he asked in sign language if I wanted the iPad. For a moment, I thought of taking it and playing Fruit Blaster or Temple Run or something. But by then, Mom had seen him gesturing to me; she stared at me and I kinda got the hint.

All these people in black gowns (I mean the lawyers) fight each other like cats and dogs. Just before Mom, it was this lady and man's turn. They walked up close to the table and stood before the lord (I mean the judge) and the two Black Gowns stood next to each of them. The lady's Black Gown said something and

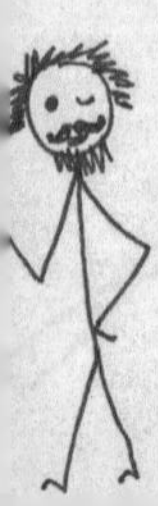

the man's Black Gown started shouting at the top of his voice. Both the Black Gowns yelled at the top of their voices. I thought they would bash each other up. The judge finally said, 'Come after a week,' and they shouted their way out of the room. It was very scary. Almost everyone was looking at them.

The judge asked me if the Man had been coming to school and scaring me.

I nodded.

The Man said I was being tutored and that the judge should talk to me alone. But the judge didn't care and asked the Man to shut up and said 'last chance' to him.

But the judge rejected Mom's appeal to have the monthly visit cancelled.

We headed straight to the children's centre.

He walked right next to me. Yeah, his beard had grown longer than last time. Taatha walked along with me, busy talking with the lawyer. Mostly, it's Taatha who talks to the lawyer.

I wanted to say sorry to the Man for lying to the judge but the Man didn't really care. He smiled cheerfully at me as if nothing had happened. He gave me his iPad. Mom would never do that.

'Do you have Temple Run in this?'

'Umm, let's download it.'

'I will go drink water.' I ran towards Mom.

'What, did he scold you?' Mom asked, concerned

I just shook my head and ran back to pick up the iPad.

The problem with the visiting centre is the moment, the Man takes something out to show me, the other kids just surround us.

There were three other boys around me giving me instructions on how to play. One tried to pull the iPad and I pulled it right back and thud! It fell down.

God, the screen cracked on the side. For a moment, I thought the Man would slap me or something. But he just made a 'Clak clak' noise and shook his head, asking me not to worry.

'Arun!' Mom called out and I ran to her.

'What, Ma?'

'How many times have I told you handle costly things with care? Did you just break that iPad?' she asked sternly.

'Only the screen has cracked. But it's working, Ma.' Mom gave me a nasty look. 'But then it's only his iPad right, not ours?' I muttered.

'Go apologise to him,' she said.

I hesitated but Mom gave me a look, so I mutely walked to the Man, who was talking with his friend.

'I am sorry,' I mumbled.

'Sorry for what?'

'For breaking the iPad.'

'Clak, clak!' He made that noise again, winked at me, and continued, 'Boss, you should try out this new game.' He handed over the iPad.

I'm sure the iPad is not his and he probably doesn't know how much it costs. Otherwise, who would keep quiet if someone breaks their iPad, right?

One of those motor-mouth boys was playing with the ball the Man had brought for me. He threw it high up and it fell on the loft over the cupboard.

I bet he did it deliberately.

Given a choice I would have punched him. Mom too was extremely annoyed. The Man asked Motor-mouth to get the ball. But he kept laughing when he talked to the boy. There was no seriousness at all.

'Come on, let me lift you and you can pick up the ball,' he told the boy.

'You threw it there, right? So you have to get it,' I added.

But Motor-mouth ran to his mom.

'Arun, let me lift you. Let's get the ball.' The Man tried lifting me.

'I won't.' I shook my head.

Know what, suddenly the Man just climbed the side of the cupboard like a monkey and was up and over it in a flash. He threw down not just my ball, but two other new tennis balls. Maybe Motor-mouth threw them one day when I wasn't there.

Mom just kept staring at the Man, expressionless. Her friend would never act like that.

I was mad at him, terribly mad. No, not for climbing up to the loft, but for throwing the other balls to Motor-mouth. Before I could get hold of them the other guys pounced on them. I think the Man should have just brought them down with him. That way, I would have had all the three balls for myself.

I hate him. I really hate him.

'Those are also mine,' I tried protesting to Motor-mouth and the other guys, but they didn't care.

If your father gets something, then it should be yours only, right?

The ball with Motor-mouth was newer than the one the Man had brought for me.

'It's cheating right, Ma? Those two guys have taken away the other two balls.'

'Go ask them. Anyway, leave it. We are not going to take anything home from here,' Mom sighed.

A policewoman walked in and saw the Man on top of the loft. I thought she would scold him or something. But she just smiled at him.

'Shall I jump down?' he asked the morons there.

'Yes!' they yelled.

'Shall I jump down, Arun?' he asked me.

I didn't reply. I guess he is mad or something. If he jumps down, I am sure he's going to fracture his leg.

'Arun, close your eyes, I'm going to jump on you. Or can you come near the cupboard? Let me climb down, stepping on your shoulders.'

Boy, the Man is irritating, he really is.

I turned away, towards Mom. Before I knew, he had climbed down by the side of the cupboard, just the way he had climbed up.

After he got down, he came to me and said, 'Pop! Pop! Pop!'

'Monkey!' I wanted to shout.

Yeah, I know it's mean.

'Come on, let me show you some magic.' He asked the kids to think of a number.

Though I tried to pretend that I was not interested at all, I watched him like an owl. Yes, I'd get a chance to show another cool trick at school!

It was this mind-reading trick where you had to think of a number and then he would ask a few questions and then write something on a piece of paper, and then continue asking questions. Finally, he'd show you the paper and bingo! It's the same number you have thought of.

He was bang on when he said that the number I thought of was '7', but I shook my head. Yeah, I couldn't help smiling. That's the problem with me.

He tickled me. 'Liar, liar.'

Yeah, it was funny, I agree.

Though I acted bored and all, he still whispered in my ear how he did the trick.

He asked me to test it out on the other kids there.

'Go ask that orange t-shirt to think of some number.'

I just shook my head.

By the way, why does he write '7' with a line on the stomach?

Know what, just as we were leaving the visiting centre, I saw the two Black Gowns who had fought like bitter enemies having tea together. I pointed them out to Mom. 'Amma, see those two lawyers, the ones who fought tooth and nail in the court. They are laughing together. See, they have become friends now.'

Mom kept staring at them.

'Can that man and lady also become friends like them?'

She didn't reply.

'Amma, will that judge also join these Black Gowns for tea?'

Mom laughed and pulled me closer to her as we walked out of the court complex.

New Trick

I didn't see him for three days at school. He generally waits at the gate. I checked out the playground, he wasn't there.

I began to feel sorry for reporting him to Mom and Taatha. I wondered if my lying to the judge had made him angry.

Was he ill or something? Or was he scared of the judge's words—'last chance'?

And then, I turned the other way and there he was, standing in a different place.

I frowned, but he was laughing heartily, and he wagged his finger at me.

I rushed into the school.

Oh yeah, I did that number magic at school. As expected, everyone went 'Ooh!' and 'Aah!'

Maths Ma'am said that it was a simple mind-maths trick.

She asked me who had taught me this.

I was silent.

'Was it your father?' she asked again.

I nodded silently.

She smiled and looked at the basketball court. But then he wasn't there or anything.

Thomas the Train

Not many get this chance. I celebrated my birthday twice this year.

The first party was thrown by Mom and her friend for me and my cousins at Pizza Corner. They gifted me a tablet. I mean, a real tablet in which I can play Angry Birds and Temple Run. It's not an iPad, though. But that's okay.

'Now you need not long for the tablet that man brings there,' Taatha said.

Mom's friend is the nicest man I know. He's always patient and answers all my questions.

Mom and Paati insist that I should call him Dad. Yes, I have started calling him Dad. Mom likes it very much. Everyone likes it.

I don't like going to birthday parties of Mom's friends' kids.

She once took me to her office friend's son's birthday party. Everyone had to go wearing coats. I wore a red coat and white pants. Know what, there was not even an inch of white space on the wall in

the living room. It was filled with pictures of the boy. I think he had been to a lot of foreign countries with his parents. There was one picture of him on a camel in some desert and one where he was playing in the snow.

His parents presented a music keyboard to him and, in turn, demanded a kiss from him.

When the parents, including Mom, moved to the other room, the boy made the other kids sit around him and started playing the keyboard.

It was damn boring so I moved towards the showcase, on top of which sat a toy train. This had a Humpty Dumpty sort of face. It was very cute.

The moment I lifted it, the music stopped. The boy ran towards me, shouting, 'Hey you!' and snatched the train from me.

'Don't you dare touch my Thomas Train!' he shouted at me.

'Where did you get this train?' one girl asked him.

'My father got it for me from the US. You won't get it here. Nobody touches any of my things here without my permission. If you want to play with Thomas Train, go ask your father to buy you one,' he barked.

I started hating the party that very instant. Why stay at a party, right, if people don't share their

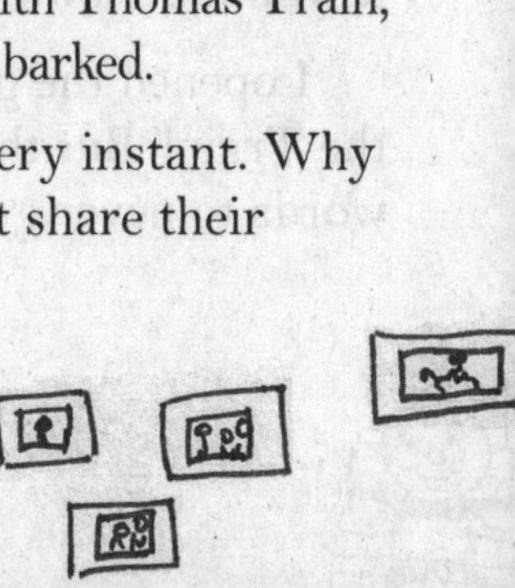

toys? However, Mom was all happy and talking with her office friends.

'Shall we go home?' I pulled at her bag.

'Two minutes, sweetie.'

'Not before eating,' the boy's mom laughed.

'I am not feeling well, Ma. I have a headache,' I whispered to Ma.

As we were leaving, Mom asked me to say goodbye to the boy.

'Bye.' I didn't even bother to look at his face.

On the way back, Mom asked me, 'Did you enjoy the party, sweetie?'

'I have a headache, Ma,' was all I said.

The second party was at the visiting centre.

Now, I didn't know there would be a party there. But the moment I stepped in, all the kids began singing 'Happy Birthday to you, Arun' and the Man took out a cake and a gift box from a bag. I thought it would be some kit for a magic show or something.

I opened the gift box and let out a cry. 'Thomas the Train!' But then I quickly remembered Paati's words to never get excited around him.

Long ago, during my second visit or so, the man had asked me, 'What do you like?' and I had mentioned Thomas the Train.

He had asked me, 'Do you want it?' and I told him it was available only in America.

I think this one's probably a duplicate. Or was it original? It did seem like an original.

'Do you like it?'

'I already have one. Mom bought it for my birthday,' I bluffed.

By now, the other kids were all over me. This Thomas the Train was really cool. Better than that boy's. You had to pour some water into a box in the bottom and turn it on and the steam came out in blue fumes. It was great.

All the other kids took turns playing with Thomas. One kid tried running the train down the slide and it came down with a thud. Mom literally jumped from her seat and gave the kid a look.

The Man was calm. He just gave a thumbs-up sign to the kid. I think it is a duplicate. Or maybe he didn't buy it. Who would keep quiet, otherwise, right?

He showed me a video of his pet dog on his iPad. It looked exactly like the one that comes in the

Vodafone ad. He called it a pug. It was cute and all, but I am afraid of dogs.

'He is eight months old,' he told me. 'When he hears the sound of my bike, some one kilometre away, he knows I'm coming and starts barking. The moment I open the gate, he goes mad,' he laughed.

In the video, the dog was jumping up and down. Know what, he was eating papaya! I didn't know that dogs ate fruits. Do they eat vegetables as well?

'What's his name?'

'I just call him Puggy. You want to name him?'

I just kept quiet and watched the video.

There was a group of kids in the play area of his apartment complex and Puggy excitedly ran towards them. The kids petted him, and as soon as they started running, the pup ran behind them, and then he was peeing on the wheel of every car and on trees and pillars.

Why did he pee so many times?

There was a group of old men sitting on a bench. Puggy went towards them and kinda sat near them and each one started petting him. One moment, he was running all excited and then the next moment he was sitting next to the old men like a good boy.

'Call him Browny,' I told the Man after a while.

He asked me if I wanted to see him and I immediately said, 'No!'

What if he took me away from Mom?

Just then, a mongrel went past the door along the verandah and the Man whistled. It turned around. He whistled again and it entered the visiting centre.

He is definitely going to be scolded by the watchman there, I thought.

The watchman wasn't around. He must have gone to have his lunch or something.

The dog slowly moved towards the Man. The Man moved his palm close to its nose and it sorta sniffed him. The Man then started rubbing its head and scratching its neck.

It looked dirty but the Man didn't seem to care. Ugh, it then started licking his hand. And know what, one other dog also came in, probably seeing its friend or something.

'Do you have some biscuits?' the Man asked me. Now the other guys had started playing with the dogs. 'Come close, they won't do anything.' I went close to him. 'See how he is wagging his tail. Do you want to touch him?'

'No.'

The other kids were petting the dogs.

'Go bring a biscuit,' he said and I ran towards Mom.

'Don't go near it,' she warned and gave me a cream biscuit while another boy came with some Britannia biscuits

The Man gave a biscuit to each of them. They finished them off in seconds and wanted more. That was the problem with them. You gave them something, they expected more.

'Pet him, pet him,' he told the boys and soon every kid was playing with the dogs. Those dogs weren't small—and one of them had some kinda wound on its back.

'Do you have some more biscuits?' he asked the guy with the Britannia buscuits. He ran back to his mom.

'Give that biscuit?' he asked me. 'Oops, chocolate cream biscuit, we can't give that. Chocolate is bad for their hearts.' He looked at me.

'I once gave a cream biscuit to one of the dogs near my house,' I told him, concerned.

'Never give them chocolate. Come near, just touch them gently. They won't do anything.' He nudged me closer to them. 'Arun, let's name them. You suggest a name.'

One was brown, the better looking one of the two, and the other was black with a wound on its back. Honestly, no one would touch them. That dirty they were. I guess the Man doesn't give much importance to cleanliness.

'Browny, Blacky,' I said and the others joined along.

'Or, should we name this one Chocolate and that one Dark Chocolate?' the Man laughed.

I laughed instantly and then quickly looked away.

One small kid tried throwing a ball at Chocolate. The Man said, 'No, no, no, no. Come here, boy, say sorry to Chocolate.'

'Come on, touch his ears. See, they're like velvet.' He held my hand and made me touch Chocolate's ears. They really were soft.

Chocolate turned around and started to lick my hand. I quickly backed away.

'It won't do anything to you, Arun.'

'Arun!' Mom shouted and ran towards me. 'I don't want to end up taking you to a doctor due to someone else's foolishness.' She dragged me towards the sofa.

Mom's probably correct.

When Mom was running towards us, the two dogs had quickly backed away.

The watchman had come back after his lunch. He chased away Chocolate and Dark Chocolate.

I am planning to name the two dogs in my street Chocolate and Dark Chocolate.

Nice-sounding names, right?

My dreams were filled with blue fumes from Thomas the Train that night.

Arm-wrestling

One good thing about going to the court is I get to travel in the flying train. Yes, it's the FLYING TRAIN that goes around the city on these overbridges.

In the mornings, the train is quite full. But on the way back, in the afternoons, it's almost empty, so I don't have a problem getting the corner seat. I mean the seat by the window. Actually, I get the whole seat. It's that empty.

Some days, when Mom's in a good mood on the way back, we sightsee together. I keep asking her, 'Ma, do you remember that roller-coaster ride at the Exhibition Grounds, when you got scared to bits? Look, the cricket stadium. Can we go to watch the cricket match there at least this year? Have you been to that temple by the sea? What's the name of that white church? Very beautiful, isn't it? Shall we get down at the Lighthouse station and go to the beach? You ride the red horse, I will ride the white; shall we see who wins? Is that red building the High Court? Is that the building where you work?'

On days when Mom's sad, she just dozes off, asking me to wake her up once we cross the computer companies.

Sometimes, I brag to my friends that I went by the flying train over the weekend. No, I don't tell them where I went.

It was 11.30 and the Man was still not in.

'We come in so early and that man doesn't turn up. That's how he is. Come on, let's leave.' Mom got up from the sofa.

Since he would definitely bring something for me to play with or have some trick up his sleeve, I told Mom that I wanted to go to the restroom, just to get more time.

I spent a good fifteen minutes in the bathroom.

'Why is it taking you this long?' Mom tapped on the door.

'Wait, Ma.' I wanted to tell her I had a stomach ache but then she would immediately ask me to leave, telling the Man that I was not feeling well. So I kept quiet.

Finally, I had to come out, but then I couldn't tell Mom that I wanted to wait for some more time to see what the Man was upto today. I just kept quiet.

'Come on, Arun,' she said and pulled my hand.

As we were about to leave, the Man ran in, panting.

Mom sighed in disappointment and went back to the sofa in the corner.

'We were about to leave,' I told the Man, without making eye contact.

'Give me two minutes. Let me catch my breath.' He was panting hard.

'Oh, I am going to have a heart attack.' He held his hand over his chest.

He winked when I looked at him, concerned.

'I thought you would have already left. I started at 11.40. Couldn't skip the meeting at office. I drove here in the traffic in ten minutes flat. Jumped two signals. There were two buses running side by side and there was this narrow gap between them; I drove through that gap. If any of the buses had applied brakes or moved any closer I would have been crushed. You should never do that, okay?

'I didn't take the entry pass to get in here. Just parked the bike in the ground and jumped the fence. One policeman shouted, "Hey, hey!" but I didn't care.'

He then showed with his hand how he had driven between the buses.

I guess he is totally reckless.

He didn't bring anything today. No Thomas the Train, no iPad, no ball.

'You didn't bring anything for me to play today.' I looked away.

'Yeah, I couldn't take anything to office. Also, I knew if I came by car, I would never reach here on time. I left the laptop in the office itself.'

Laptop? Does he also work for some computer company like Mom?

'Have you been to the US?' Though I knew the answer would be no, I asked the Man.

'Umm, let's see, touch one of these two fingers.'

I touched his index finger, irritated.

'Then yes, I have been to the US.'

'Have you been to London?' I asked after some time.

'Umm, touch one of these two fingers.'

I touched the other finger this time.

'Then no, I haven't been to London.'

I doubt if he ever speaks the truth.

Even as we were talking, he put his arm under my shirtsleeve and pulled hard, and there was this loud pop sound.

'Pop! Pop! Pop!' he went. 'Come on, try on my sleeve.'

'No, I don't want to.'

Then he pulled the shirt of another boy with a military style-haircut who was sitting next to him and the pop sound amused the boy to bits.

It worked not only on clothes; the Man was able to make the pop sound by pulling the edge of the bench, the chair, almost anything.

I tried to find out if he had something in his hand to make the sound.

'Come on, try out on my shirt,' he encouraged Military Boy, who almost tore the sleeve off the Man's shirt.

'No, no, not like that.'

He put his hand on my sleeve and pulled. I frowned.

'Pop! Pop! Pop! Pops, pops, pops!' He annoyed me.

Now that kid was going around pulling the other kids' shirts.

As the kid moved away, he said, 'You don't need to pull anybody's shirt to do this trick.'

'Just hold your left thumb this way.' He held his left thumb with his index finger. 'Now using the middle finger of your right hand, pull it hard. There you go: Pop! Pop, pop, pop! Pops, pops, pops!'

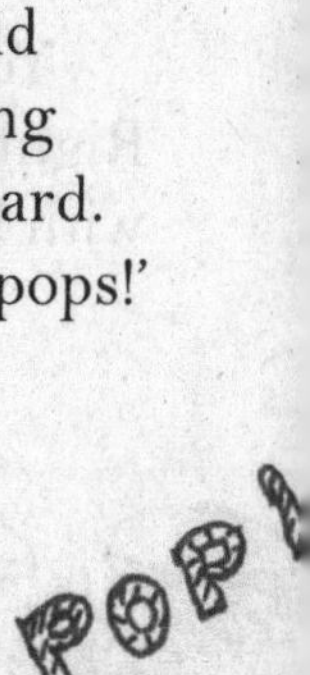

Though I was interested as hell, I just kept looking the other way. I never look in his direction when I speak. When he talks to me, I look at the wall.

'Never make eye contact with him. He will probably cast some spell on you,' Paati had warned me. Yeah, I don't want to take any chances.

Mom was busy talking to Laptop Lady. This lady, who always comes with her laptop, is the only person Mom talks to. Her son Rahul (yeah, Mom told me his name, I don't talk to him) keeps eating all the time and never joins the other boys. But then he seems thin for the amount of eating he does. If he's bored of eating, he takes his mom's phone and keeps staring at the screen. Not sure what game he plays.

Mom told me that the lady works for some computer company. I've never seen her husband, though. I think he never turns up.

She comes to court by car.

Mom had introduced me to her once.

'Which standard, smarty?' she asked me. 'Rahul, give our new friend a cookie.'

You should have seen Mobile Canteen's face then. Right then, I decided I was never going to be friends with him. Ever!

I wonder if her laptop bag contains the laptop or snacks for the boy.

Never mind!

The Man sat beside me quietly. I guess he was trying to catch his breath or something.

Suddenly, he said, 'You know what, I can touch my nose with my tongue. Can you do that? Let me see if your tongue is as long as mine.'

I kept looking at the wall.

He asked a boy who just walked in, 'How long is your tongue? Can you touch your nose with it?'

The boy giggled.

'See.' The Man touched his nose with his tongue.

The boy sitting next to him went ha-ha-ha.

The boy who had just come in tried but he wasn't able to.

The Man was sweating and his shirt almost seemed drenched.

Mom's friend would never come that way to my house. He always smells good. This Man smelt of sweat.

The Man said, 'See, my beard has grown longer than last time, right? How do I look?'

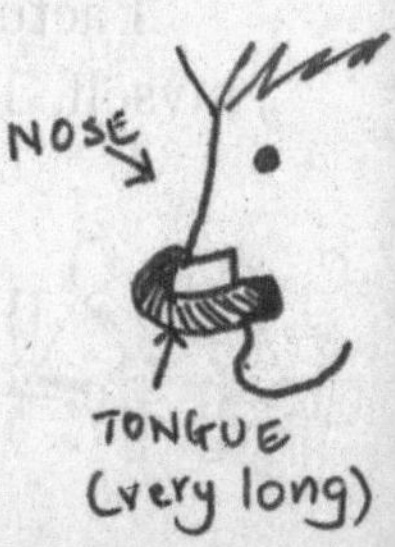

'Ugly,' I said and looked away.

He laughed heartily.

'Come on, tell me once more, Arun. How do I look?' he asked again, muffling his laugh.

'Ugly.'

Now would you laugh if someone called you ugly? I guess there is something wrong with the Man.

'Come, let's arm-wrestle.' He was irritating me again.

I kept staring at the lazing leopard on the wall.

'Hey, do you want to arm-wrestle?' he asked the guy with dirty teeth who always kept watching both of us to see what we were up to.

'Yes!' he yelled.

Two other guys, one with ear studs and the other with Harry Potter specs, joined along and they together defeated the man.

'Arun, can you help me defeat these chaps?' the Man asked me.

Even before I could reply, Dirty Teeth pulled my arm.

I actually didn't want to but then I couldn't stop myself. The other kids surrounded us.

The Ear Stud and Harry-Potter Specs took Dirty Teeth's side, cheering for him, while the Man cheered for me.

I almost lost. But then, in a final-ditch effort, I gritted my teeth and pushed the guy's hand with all my might and flattened him. There was a big roar as everyone around cheered loudly.

Mom shut her ears with her hands, showing her annoyance.

The Man lifted my hand the way the referee lifts the hand of the winner in a boxing match, and started shouting 'Champion! Champion!' like this Bravo guy of Chennai Super Kings.

By now, even the dads of some of the guys joined along.

I smiled and looked at Mom. But she wasn't amused.

'Boy, you are really strong. You really are.' The Man felt my muscles. 'What do you eat?'

'I attend karate class.' I looked away.

'Wow, wow, you are a Karate Kid. Excellent!' he laughed. 'Hello Karate Kid! Karate Kid! Do you know there's this movie called *Karate Kid*? Boy, call Arun Karate Kid from now on, okay?' he told Dirty Teeth.

Karate Kid! Yeah, I like the name. Nice-sounding one, isn't it?

'Can we arm-wrestle once, just once?' he kept asking me.

I just shook my head and stole a glance at Mom. I think I can easily beat the Man. After all, he lost to Dirty Teeth, while I defeated him.

Back home, I tried a few karate moves with Taatha, who laughed hysterically.

'I am Karate Kid. Mind it!' I threatened him.

Yeah, Karate Kid. I like the name.

That night, Mom got me a cake from McRennett bakery. Butterscotch. She mockingly put a small dot of cream under my nose.

Yeah, I was able to reach that cream with my tongue.

Lucky Mom

Mom's friend took us out to the Crown Plaza hotel today. It is the biggest hotel I have ever been to. You know, it's a five-star hotel.

Mom was dressing up for like an hour before we started. 'Arun, wear the new jeans that we bought at the mall and that jacket we purchased for Shreya's wedding.'

Taatha and Paati came along with us.

'Please wear shoes, Pa. They won't allow people without shoes,' Mom told Taatha.

'Ma, should Paati also wear shoes with her sari?' I asked her and everyone went ha-ha-ha.

'Eat decently, Arun. Don't lick the plate or your fingers,' Taatha said.

Mom's friend has got a promotion, or something. He will be making frequent trips abroad.

'Arun, you will now be getting lots and lots of chocolates and toys,' Mom beamed.

He came with flowers for Mom and a bouquet for Paati as well. He was dressed like these models that come in shirting & suiting ads on TV. That smart.

He was wearing a jacket and shiny black shoes.

He brought me a box of chocolates, yeah, foreign chocolates.

When you get down from the car, they take the car key and go park it somewhere. It was not as crowded as the regular restaurants we generally visit.

We entered a big hall. It looked like a palace. Mom and I took a selfie near the fountain at the centre.

From the outside, you could not smell the food or see people eating. Usually, when we get into a restaurant, there's a lot of noise, right? Here there was pin-drop silence and many people were wearing coats.

I wanted to go the restroom and Taatha accompanied me.

Wow, I've never seen a restroom like that. The floor was so clean that I could easily sleep on it. They had these scented candles (I mean, the fat ones) lit everywhere inside the restroom and it smelt sweet, unlike my school restroom.

There were a lot of paintings hanging everywhere in the hotel, and even the men who served food looked very smart.

Taatha took the menu card and quickly passed it on to Mom's friend, saying, 'Looking at the prices, I am going to get a heart attack.'

As we had dinner, Mom's friend spoke to Taatha about the kind of work he would be doing now. Mom joined the conversation.

'That's how a gentleman should behave,' Taatha told me later.

'Your mother is very lucky,' Paati said.

Mom is very lucky, yeah!

Split Eyebrow

I broke my jaw yesterday. Well, almost. As I ran up the staircase during the recess, I tripped and fell and bang! My jaw hit the step. I bet someone knocked me down from behind.

The next thing I knew, there was blood dripping down my face and I almost fainted. I started crying. The class teacher held a cloth to my jaw to stop the blood while the ayah ran to bring some ice. The teacher then called up Mom.

You should have seen Mom! She rushed in as if I had had a heart attack or something.

She took me to this hospital very close to my school, and the doctor cleaned the cut with some liquid that made it burn like he had set fire to it. He also gave me an injection. Then all I could remember was Mom standing outside while he used a needle and thread to stitch the wound. Four stitches, to be exact.

Mom cried and called her friend, who rushed to the hospital.

After the stitches, I kinda felt less pain except when I touched the bandage. Mom kept asking me, 'Is it hurting you, baby?'

This morning, Mom told me, 'If it is hurting you, let's not go, baby.'

'It's okay, Ma.'

I wondered how the Man would react seeing my bandaged jaw. Had the principal or PT Sir already informed him of my injury?

Would you believe it, he laughed when he saw me! I immediately wanted to return home. He's so cruel.

'What happened? Did you get involved in a fight or something?'

I didn't say anything.

'What happened?' he nudged me.

I was in no mood to answer. 'I fell down.'

'Actually, it's cool, Arun. Having battle scars is cool, isn't it? See my left eyebrow. Do I have a split eyebrow?' he asked me

I stole a glance and then looked away.

'When I was in eleventh standard, I still remember, we were having this cricket tournament. It was the semifinals and I tried hooking a short ball and the ball—the hard cricket ball—struck me on my eyebrow. It instantly cut the eyebrow into two and blood started gushing down my face. Everyone rushed towards me, the fielders, the umpires,

everyone. I don't remember clearly now, but I think one of the guys pressed a handkerchief hard on the cut to stop the bleeding while my coach poured water over it.

'I remembered when my hero, Sachin Tendulkar, was sixteen, he had taken a blow on his nose from Pakistani fast bowler Waqar Younis, but bravely battled on.

'I wanted to be like him, so I told my coach, I will bat on. Also, a couple of girls from my school were watching the match so I wanted to come across as a brave kid.

'"Don't be foolish. We need to rush to the hospital," the coach shouted.

'"No sir, I am alright, I want to bat," I kept saying stubbornly. Finally, he had no option except to leave the field.

'I batted on and scored a fifty. It is a different story that we lost the match. News spread amongst the boys and girls that I was one brave kid.

'You should have seen the look on the faces of the girls of my grade when I entered class with the bandage.' He laughed like a kid.

I stole a glance at his split eyebrow again and then looked away.

'Now that you will have a scar, when you grow big, you can narrate your act of bravery to your girlfriend. But remember, don't tell her that you tripped down the stairs. Instead, tell her that you got into a fight with a guy who messed with some weak person on the street,' he winked

I tried to hide my smile by looking away.

I guess the Man is a crackpot or something.

Mom was looking at me intently.

I'm sure Taatha will get mad if I tell him what the Man told me.

There was a big fight at the visiting centre today.

One lady was holding on to her daughter, who had two ladybird clips on her head. The Ladybird Girl's father wanted to meet her but she refused to leave her mom. Neither would her mom allow her to go.

I'd never seen the girl before; it's probably their first visit to the centre. I think she must be in second standard, just like me. She's shorter than me, though.

The father tried pulling the Ladybird Girl towards him, and both the lady and the girl cried. He then brought the police lady, who asked the lady to go away from the centre, leaving the girl with him.

The lady was in no mood to budge. She held on to the girl tightly and they sat in a corner, both of them, just beside the window, like lizards stuck to the wall. The policewomen tried talking to the lady and then tried forcibly taking away the Ladybird Girl from her. But she wouldn't let go of the kid.

'Even if I die, I won't leave you,' the lady told the Ladybird Girl.

I doubt if Mom would ever act like that, with everybody watching.

Finally, the father went out and came with more policemen, lawyers and the judge, and a crowd gathered outside to watch the happenings.

'Move! Move!' the policewomen ordered as the judge came in. The judge tried asking the lady to leave the kid and wait outside, but still the lady wouldn't budge. The judge saw me and the Man, and she told the lady, 'See this kid and his father, how happily they are playing!' The lady didn't care.

The policewoman tried forcing the lady outside but she howled loudly (I mean the lady). Then the Ladybird Girl started howling too. It was scary as hell.

No matter who talked to her—lawyer, judge or the policewoman—the lady wouldn't budge.

Finally, the judge had to tell the father to be patient. But then he started shouting too, so for a few moments the whole place was like a battlefield.

'Shall we go sit outside till this thing ends?' the Man asked me.

I wanted to go out, too. There was so much noise. I checked with Ma but she was busy watching the fight and didn't want to move.

After some time, the Ladybird Girl's dad accompanied the judge to the court. Even after that, the lady sat in the corner, holding on to the kid tightly.

I continued watching the Ladybird Girl for some time. She sat in the tight grip of her mom and slowly fell asleep. None of the ladies went to talk to her mom.

The Laptop Lady wasn't there today. I asked Mom about her.

'She will not be coming anymore.'

'Why?'

'Because she and her husband have agreed to end their fighting and live together. Happily ever after,' she said after a pause

'You will feel bored here, right? ' I asked her.

'I hate this place.'

'Me too,' I said.

Maths Ma'am called me to solve a problem and I wrote '7' with a line on the stomach.

Yeah, I've started writing the number 7 with a line on the stomach; I guess I am the only guy in class who writes it that way. It just seems cool, doesn't it?

I had a sudden thought: did the Man ever narrate his split eyebrow story to Mom?

I need to ask her.

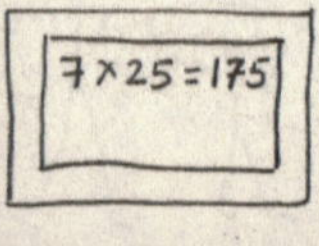

Vroom! Vroom!

I don't think we will be going to court anymore. Mom petitioned the court to change the place of meeting from that visiting centre to some place that's closer to home.

I guess she wanted it changed for two reasons.

1. Mom wanted the visit to happen closer home so that we wouldn't have to go so far.
2. She wanted to forget the court and the fights she had been through there. She said she views that phase of life as a bad dream and wants to forget it fast.

Good that Mom asked for a change of place. It's kinda very stuffy sitting there and staring at the walls with monkeys and peacocks and policemen and all the fathers visiting their kids and people fighting and that Running Nose guy and that girl and mom who keep reading and reading.

Mom expected a fight from the Man, but he readily agreed. But then he suggested Xpress Mall, instead of the park close to home that Taatha had suggested.

Taatha's disappointed. But I am happy. I love Xpress Mall.

The mall's huge with a lot of shops and this wide food court and the cinema where Mom, her friend and I watched *Spiderman* recently. I like going to the theatre. The theatre is huge and the popcorn there is great. I go there for the popcorn. Mom's friend bought me this double-decker ice cream from Baskin Robbins. It was just amazing.

Know what, the theatre has these pushback seats, where you can watch the movie almost lying flat. Also, they serve popcorn right at your seat itself, that too when the movie is going on.

The Xpress Mall—you have every shop there: Hamleys, Baskin Robbins, Subway, Pizza Corner, Starbucks. I've been there four times, twice with Mom and a couple of times with my cousins.

Mom goes quite often to Big Bazaar where everyone buys groceries and everything else they need for the house. I bought my birthday clothes there.

Then there's FunCity; that's where all the kids like to go. There are a million choices there; lots of video games.

I like that go-karting track that's just outside FunCity but then Mom says it's too costly and too risky as well.

Anyway, she will never drive along with me.

I hopped my way into the mall, with Mom. Mom told me to be on my guard all the time.

There was music blaring all around. But still, it is much better than that dingy visiting room at the centre.

The Man was already there.

Even before the Man could ask where I wanted to go, I said, 'Let's go to FunCity.'

With the Man, I decide what I want. There's no way I can do that with Mom.

As we went up the escalator, the Man asked if I wanted to go to the Ghost House.

Yeah, I've always wanted to go there but then Mom's afraid of scary movies so she always says sternly, 'Nothing doing.'

I could go and brag in school that I just walked through the Ghost House without getting scared, right?

'No Arun, no!' Mom pulled my shirt.

'Please, Ma,' I begged.

Mom also came along so that I wouldn't get scared or something.

And before I knew it, we were in this dark place with spooky noises and skeletons suddenly dancing

around and mummies jumping up from the coffins. Boy, it is spooky. It really is.

The Man tried holding my hand; I pushed it away and held Mom's. It's like a secret tunnel or something that winds and winds around with some spooky thing waiting to scare us at every corner.

As we entered this passage called 'River of Blood', it smelt like it was infested with bats. There were even some screeching sounds. Suddenly, a lion on the wall opposite to the passage starting spitting at me and there was something crawling all over my feet. I jumped. It seemed like cockroaches or spiders or something.

'Ma, Ma, pick me up. Lift me!' I shouted and the Man tried lifting me, but Mom and I ran from the spot as fast as we could and climbed the stairs, which suddenly started moving. Very scary!

We continued running until we were at the exit and the Man came out behind us, grinning.

'Did you like it, Arun?'

'I hate it! Shall we go home?' I checked with Mom. I was too spooked.

'Spend twenty more minutes with him, then we shall leave. I should have warned you that he is reckless,' Mom whispered.

Yeah, this Ghost House kinda spooked me too much.

We headed to FunCity.

There were a million kids at the FunCity. The little ones tumbled out of the Ball-Zone while many others were playing these 3D video games.

'What do you want to play?'

I showed him the virtual helicopter ride. I knew it cost a lot because when I had asked Mom the last time, she just said, 'I don't want to waste so much money on this ride.' I decided to ask the Man for the costliest rides.

Know what, he just said, 'Come, let's ride.'

In this ride, you sit in a chair with belts and all, and they put these glasses on you. Then the chair starts to move. The glass has a video screen that makes you feel you're riding in a helicopter through the mountains and over oceans and between the valleys.

'I am going to fall down. I am going to fall down. Save me, save me, Arun! Hold my hand, I am falling!' the Man kept shouting. I just ignored him.

We then tried out the Hammer Blow, where you hit the base hard with a hammer and a sorta pointer moves up. I hit it once and the pointer didn't move up by a lot. I just got three points.

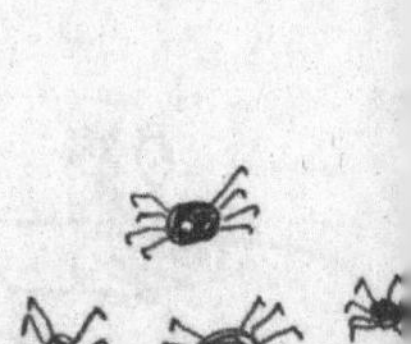

'Let me try.' The Man hit the base with all his might and the pointer went up to thirty-two.

'Ten more minutes, Arun.' Mom pointed to her watch.

'It was very exciting when we came here last time, right?' she asked me when I went to drink water.

I went back.

'Come, let's go-kart.' I knew for sure that it was very expensive and that he would say no.

Would you believe it, he just said, 'Yes, let's go.'

'No, Arun!' Mom shouted.

'It's okay, I will take care of him.' That was the first time I ever saw the Man talking to Mom.

The go-karting track is actually outside FunCity in the open yard. They even have these floodlights there.

'Which car do you want?' he asked me.

'The red one.'

'You mean the Ferrari?'

'The red one,' I repeated.

'You the driver, or me?' he asked.

'I will drive.'

'See, this is the accelerator. You keep pressing this and it will go fast. This is the brake; when you see the barriers just turn around or apply the brakes. To reverse, just push the pedal back. Got it?'

I didn't reply.

'Come on, Arun, take your pick. Whom do you want to race against? That girl or that boy?'

I didn't answer.

When the bell went off, I wasn't quite able to start and he kept saying, 'Press the accelerator. Press it, Arun!' Then he pulled the steering and the car began to move. 'Press it hard Arun.'

But I was pushing the pedal backward, instead of forward, and the car was not going anywhere. 'Didn't I tell you press it hard and forward?'

Just then, one of the boys in a red Vodafone t-shirt sped past me and put his tongue out at me.

My car started moving slowly, very slowly. I was riding the Ferrari like a bicycle or something.

'Press it hard, Arun!' the Man kept shouting.

The Vodafone t-shirt came around for the second round to race me and he hit my car from behind. He showed a thumbs-down sign and rode away fast.

'Loser, loser!' he shouted.

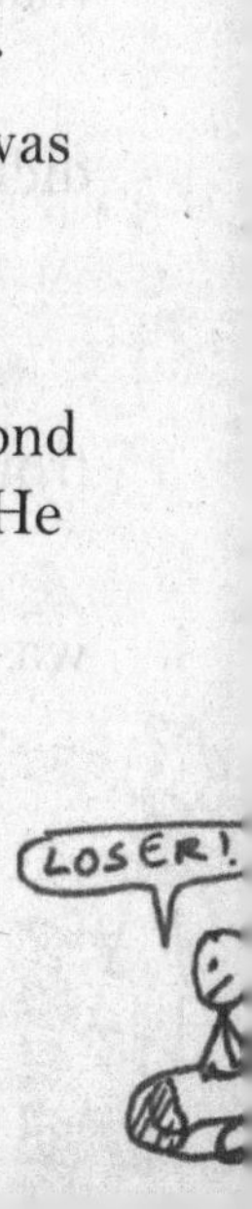

'It's okay, Arun. We are doing great,' the Man told me as I completed the round.

As we were getting out of the car, Vodafone t-shirt walked past me and shouted 'Loser!' again.

He was much bigger than me. Probably in the eighth standard or something

I guess the boy had taken a full-day pass, because he again got into one of the cars.

'Come on, Arun, let's show him who we are,' the Man said.

Mom shouted from outside, 'Arun, its time, let's go.'

'Arun, let's do it one more time. Let's show that boy what we are made of. Just pretend that you didn't hear your mom.'

'I want to change cars. This isn't good. Let's take that orange car.'

'Fine! Jump into that car and pretend that you didn't hear your mom.'

He went to pay while I fastened the seat belt.

Mom kept shouting 'Arun, didn't you hear me?' from outside the fence.

I ignored Mom and kept looking at the boy. He was making faces at me.

'Come on, you drive,' I told the Man.

'No, you are driving; let's smoke that boy this time. Let's make a plan. You press the pedal hard and I will control the steering, okay?'

I just nodded.

The bell went off again and the Vodafone t-shirt immediately sped past me.

'Arun, just keep pressing the pedal,' the Man said.

I kept pressing and somehow the car wouldn't move. Whichever car I get into seems to have some problem.

The man then put his leg from across the seat and pressed the pedal while controlling the steering with his right hand.

Our car slowly began to move. By now, that guy's car was way ahead of us.

And then, our car began to slowly gain speed.

'Arun, now we are going to have fun!' the Man shouted.

We swung around one of the cars, just missing it, and bumped against the tyre barrier.

'You are pressing my leg hard,' I told him.

'Take your leg off the accelerator. Move it to one side.'

He pressed hard on the pedal and the car really took off. There we were, overtaking one car after the other. But then, two of the cars blocked our passage before we could take on Vodafone t-shirt.

'You are riding well, Arun. Keep it up. That's it!' the Man kept shouting.

Two cars, the pink one driven by a kid with his grandfather, and the yellow one by this bespectacled boy, were going slow and there was a narrow gap between them. They were blocking our way, so we couldn't take on Bad Guy.

'Yes, let's drive fast and go between the two,' I shouted. We drove like mad between the two cars, hitting both of them out of our way, and surged ahead.

We were now closing in on the boy.

'Push, faster, faster!' I shouted to the Man. The boy looked back and saw us.

'Arun, now let's show the boy who we are! Do you want to dash against his car?'

'YES!' I squealed.

'There you go!'

Our car surged ahead like a real race car and hit Bad Guy's car from the side and made it spin off the track and into the barricade.

'YES! YES! YES!' I shouted.

The Man held out his hand. 'Give me a high-five, Arun, you drove really fast.'

I high-fived him.

'We make a great team! We are the Chennai Super Kings!'?' the Man exclaimed.

I guess so.

I looked back at Bad Guy. Oh yeah, he was both disappointed and angry.

My heart was thumping as we crossed the finish line and I kept glancing over at the boy.

'Hey, let's race one more time. I'll see that you lose badly this time,' the boy called out to me.

I shook my head and walked towards the gate.

'One day we will buy a full-day ticket and keep driving and driving, okay?' the Man commented.

'Umm. Don't waste your time outside the school gates tomorrow. We have rehearsal for the play I am acting in. It's on Tuesday at the University Hall.'

'Will they allow everyone?'

'No, they won't. They will only allow those with valid passes.'

'Can you get me a pass?'

I shook my head.

'I will be there. From the stage, look around in the audience, I will be there in one of the aisles waving a white handkerchief at you,' he laughed.

'They won't let you in,' I repeated.

'We'll see. What time?' he asked.

'5 pm.'

As I came out of the gate, I couldn't see Mom and suddenly my excitement gave way to fear.

'Ma, Ma!' I started looking around. My old fears returned—that the Man would take me away.

'Cool, Arun. I have your mom's phone number. We can call if we are not able to find her.'

My heart slowly went back to beating normally.

The moment Mom saw me, she grabbed my hand and dragged me away with her.

'Bad manners! Disrespecting elders! Recklessness! That's what you will learn if you spend time with bad men. Are you deaf? Didn't you hear me calling your name at least a thousand times?' she shouted as she dragged me away.

As I walked down the stairs, I looked up, and there he was at the top of the stairs, waving his hand at me.

'Like father, like son. Unruly,' Mom remarked.

Like father, like son!

The Play

The play we were doing was called *Whodunit.* I was playing the role of a policeman. A lady gets robbed of her chain and I investigate and find out the culprit.

How do I find the thief? Well, that's the story.

Mom made me rehearse at least a thousand times. She made me recite my lines to Paati, Taatha, and then to her friend.

Mom's friend corrected my pronunciation of some of the words. He showed me how to pronounce the British way and the American way. Paati watched in awe.

'You should definitely be there for the play,' she told him.

'I will try my best, Auntie. Ninety-nine per cent I will be there.'

'Hundred per cent,' Mom replied in a mock-stern tone.

Mom's friend took a selfie with Mom and me.

'Arun, do a good job. After the play gets over, let's all celebrate at some cool restaurant.'

I even rehearsed once wearing the new outfit (I mean the police khakis). The pants were quite long and had to be folded three times. But then Mom said that I would anyway grow fast and so the length need not really be altered. But her friend wanted it to be perfect to make it a perfect occasion.

I fully agreed with him. Yeah, he is a very intelligent man.

He gave me his dark glasses and said I would look great with the glasses on, as almost all cops in movies wear fancy glasses.

'But handle them carefully. They cost fifteen thousand rupees,' he said.

'Oops, you mad or what? I will buy him a cheaper pair,' Mom said.

Taatha examined the glasses with care.

'Arun, don't look at the audience at all. Not at any of us. Not at Mom, not at Paati or me. You'll get tense and fumble your lines. Just look at the other actors on the stage. Just think you are playing to an empty house,' he advised.

'Try spotting me in the audience. I will be there,' the Man had challenged.

Should I look around or not?

The Annual Day

I'm not sure how I got selected to play the policeman, who is the hero of the play. They had this selection where each one of us was made to say a few lines like 'I can identify a thief by looking at a person's eyes' and a few other dialogues I don't quite remember now.

It was the guys whose parents that regularly attend the PTA meetings who generally got selected; but this time Maths Ma'am wanted me to play the role.

It was between Krish, whose Mom keeps visiting the school every other day, and me. English Ma'am wanted Krish to play the policeman's role while Maths Ma'am said I would suit the role better as I was slightly big (yeah, I hate the word fat). English Ma'am argued that I was very quiet by nature and might not do well, but Maths Ma'am said she was confident that I would fit the part well.

I never thought I would get selected; actually I would have been happy even if I had been selected to play one of the thieves.

I guess I should thank Maths Ma'am for selecting me.

We have had a million rehearsals at school, so by now I can say everybody else's dialogues as well. I do that just to amuse Mom, Pa and Paati.

Paati joked that the Man can train me well to play a thief, but Mom asked her to stop it.

The nicest thing about being selected for the Annual Day play was that I could skip a lot of classes because we were always rehearsing. Yeah, I didn't need to worry about slip tests for a few days.

The bad thing was I needed to do a lot of catching up at home, like copying the notes or doing the lessons with Taatha.

The day before the play, we had final practice in the actual auditorium. I had a good time in the bus where the fifth-grade kids, who were acting in a different play, sang songs and Ma'am made a few of them dance as well.

Maths Ma'am asked if I could dance and I shook my head.

I sat next to Pooja, who played the woman whose chain gets snatched by the thief in the play. She also danced.

'You dance well,' I told her.

'I attend dance class every weekend.'

'Oh.'

She is from a different section. She is very nice. She even shared her sandwich. She didn't shout when I accidently spilt water on her when I drank from the water bottle.

She said her father is very excited about her acting in the play, and has created a small video of her practising. Seems like her father is purchasing her an electric scooter (I mean an actual mini-scooter) as a gift. Her mom has bought her matching earrings, socks and even nail polish just for the play.

'Are your parents coming?' she asked me.

'Of course my Mom is coming. My grandparents as well.'

'Your dad?'

'He's busy; he will not be able to come.'

'You got hurt or something?' She pointed to my chin.

'No, I fought with a guy near my house who tried to grab my friend's bag,' I bluffed.

I remembered the Man.

'Oh, that's why I guess you got selected to play the cop.'

Know what, she thought I was telling the truth.

We had to take our costumes to school, and from school they would take us to the auditorium. We would change into our costumes there.

'Do well, baby. You are going to make us proud.' Mom kissed me.

Her friend called and wished me.

'Ma, when will you be there?' I checked with Mom.

'Much before the play starts. I will come and dress you up, sweetie.'

'No Ma, Ma'am will do that. The principal asked us not to bring our parents backstage.'

'Drink water so that you don't get thirsty. And have biscuits so that you don't feel hungry or something.'

'Ma'am said they will bring cakes and juice for us,' I beamed.

I remembered a story the Man told me while we were looking for Mom Xpress Mall.

'When I was younger than you—I think I was in first grade—I acted in this play, *Little Boy Blue.* I wore a blue coat and matching pants and a blue hat. After the teachers dressed me up and all, they turned their attention to the other actors. I wanted to go to the restroom, and since all teachers I knew had left the room, I was scared to ask the PT Miss who was very strict and always shouting instructions. The

urge started getting stronger by the minute. On top of that, they distributed juice, which was impossible for me to resist.

'And then my bladder started to disobey. I started losing control. My pants started turning blue—a tell-tale wet dark blue. And the moment I went on stage, everyone laughed their hearts out. After that, all I remember is everyone at home laughing at me.

'So don't forget to go to the restroom twenty minutes before the play, otherwise you know what I mean, right?' The Man had laughed and scratched my neck.

I hid a smile as I got into the bus.

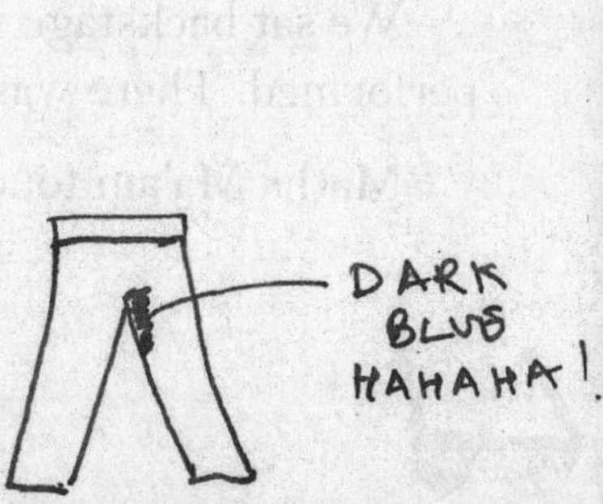

Clak! Clak!

Ma'am applied powder on my face and, know what, she even applied lipstick. I'm not sure why they put lipstick on me. For quite a long time, I didn't close my mouth at all.

I had already tried out the police uniform at home along with the cap, and Mom had given me her friend's dark glasses.

'Don't lose them, mind you,' she had said sternly. 'In case Ma'am doesn't allow you to wear them, ask her to call me.'

'Oh, you are the one playing the cop,' one of the ladies who had come to apply make-up for us commented.

We could hear the principal giving her opening speech. 'Please don't stand up or film the performance on your mobile. We will be giving the CD of the entire function to all those who want it,' she finished.

We sat backstage while the fifth-standard group performed. There was a big roar from the audience.

Maths Ma'am touched up our faces one last time.

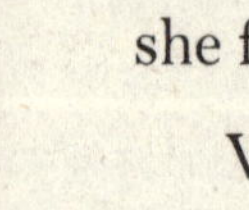

'Good luck, children. Do well.'

'Are you tense?' Pooja asked me.

I did 'Clak! Clak!' and shook my head. 'You?' I asked.

'I am nervous.'

As we were talking, there was loud applause.

'First- and second-grade kids, get ready,' Maths Ma'am shouted.

I felt the urge to go to the restroom. But I kept quiet.

The auditorium was full. We had to move forward towards the mic to mouth our dialogues. English Ma'am would prompt each of us to go on stage.

'Go Pooja.'

'Arun, your turn.'

Pooja's dad whistled loudly when she went on stage. It was very funny.

The vice-principal kept prompting from the side.

I went on stage with the dark glasses on. People clapped. The only problem was, I couldn't see properly. So I removed them and put them in my pocket.

Nobody fumbled their dialogues.

There was this identification parade where all the suspects were made to line up and I had to find the culprit by looking at their eyes.

'Is he the culprit?'

'No.'

'Is he the culprit?'

I did 'Clak! Clak!', and shook my head. There was thunderous applause.

Know what, every line I said, people laughed and clapped. It had never happened to me before.

When I was done with all my lines, I looked up at the audience. I found Mom in the second row along with her friend, Paati and Pa, smiling broadly. She gestured to me to put my glasses on.

I looked around to the left side and then to the right.

And there he was, in the corner, would you believe it? The Man, waving his white handkerchief at me, just as he had told me he would.

How had he got in?

I stole a glance in his direction again, and he gave me a thumbs-up and waved his handkerchief again.

The play ended with everyone clapping for a long time.

As the curtains came down, Maths Ma'am asked, 'What's this "Clak! Clak!"? Very stylish!'

I just smiled.

Mom ran backstage to pick me up; she kissed me and said that I had acted fabulously.

The parents of many of the kids did the same. Mom gave me a Cadbury Fruit & Nut bar, my favourite.

Pooja's father took a picture of all of us backstage. I put the glasses on and took a picture with Mom. It was very funny.

I offered a piece of the chocolate to Pooja and she went 'Clak! Clak!' and everyone laughed their hearts out.

'Who taught you this?' Mom asked me, laughing.

I just held my left thumb with my finger and pulled it. It went POP!

I am V. Arun. I am eight years old

My father's name is Venkatesh. He is very good He never gets mad at me. He takes me to Xpress Mall where we Go-kart. He buys me a lot of toys and chocolates. He got me Thomas the Train for my birthday. We watch movies and sports together. He teaches me cricket and car racing. He loves dogs.

I love my Pops.